homeless

by Mike Boyce

Tips for teachers on how to use this book
Homelessness is a sensitive issue, many schools and families in public schools today are impacted by this issue, when discussing with your students, be mindful that your students may be having this experience, and to be sensitive about how you ask questions, and lead discussions.

This book is dedicated to Diane Dick, Kathleen Bomze, Julia Popowitz, Ed Belmonte, Brian Woods, Don King, Mara Skov, Robert Boyce, Lauren Bida, Laura Kenney, Bianca Crampton, Valerie Dadante, Morenike O'Neal, Midge Wilson, Keistian Simsarian, Ron Chan, Taro Hattori, Cheryl Zelina, Vikki Del Rosario, Saraleah Fordyce, Erik Adigard, Matthew Silady, Allison Smith, Doug Lenhart, Maria Makela, Pallavi Sharma, Ruben Speers, Karina O'Neill, Shalini Agrawal, Monique Butler, Jonathan Massey, Jeannine Szamreta, Janeece Hayes, Thomas Eusterbrock, Michelle Lewis, Melissa Leventon, Juan Hernandez, Michelle Wadleigh, Rachel Berger, Jon Stich, Kent Griffin, Kevin McCloskey, Erin Newman, Owen Smith, GoFundMe Team, Linda Currie, Teresa Sal, Joseph McGinnis, Kye Bach, Vickie Peng, Aylin Aybar, Cynthia Lyons-Dailard, Cathy Hobart, Susan Derfus, Erin Collins, Bernadette Armbruster, Bookbaby and everyone trying to make a difference in this complex world.

My name is Chris. I live with Mommy, Daddy, and baby Sam.

This is my home. I have my own room
with stars on the ceiling.

My mommy reads me a bedtime story every night.

This is my school, my favorite subject is reading.
I like my teacher, Mister Jane.

One day we had to move out of our home.
I had to pick one toy. I picked Bear.

We moved in with Aunt Sandy across the Bay.

We all shared a room.
Mommy read me a bedtime story every night.

It was exciting to take the train to school,
but it took a really long time.

Getting up so early was very hard.
I started to fall asleep in class.

Mister Jane asked to meet with Mommy.

We had to move out of Aunt Sandy's house.
She did not have room for us anymore.

We moved into a motel.

Mommy met with Mister Jane.
He told her about a place that helps families.

The motel was very noisy and small.

Mommy read me a bedtime story every night.

I went with Mommy to the place that helps families and we waited in a long, long line.

We were put on a list because there are lots of families that are homeless and need help.

At school Jesse invited me to a birthday party,
but I didn't go because I couldn't buy a present.

We ran out of money and had to move out of the motel and into our car.

From our car I looked at the stars and thought
about my old room.

There were lots of people without homes.
Just like us.

Bear was cold and scared so I wrapped my blanket around her to keep her warm, and I told her it was going to be OK.

I spent a lot of time at the library. I like to read books, and sometimes I had nowhere else to go.

We met with Miss Jack. She is a social worker
who was helping us find a home.

We went to a church and slept on
the floor with other homeless families.
Mommy read me a bedtime story
every night.

We moved into a special place for families without homes called a shelter.

It has many bunk beds
and a bathroom
that we all share.

Then we got to move into our very own room at the shelter, with our own bathroom! Bear was happy.

Mommy read me a bedtime story every night.

Finally we get our own home again,
with my very own room!

Daddy paints stars on the ceiling of my new room.

At night when I stare at the stars, I remember when I didn't have a home and I am thankful because not everyone has a home.

THE END

Are you looking for homeless resources in your area?

Volunteers of America (800-899-0089)

HUD National Hotline (877-424-3838)

The Salvation Army (1-800-728-7825)

visit www.homelessshelterdirectory.org

Visit www.mikeboyce.com for more books like this.